Codependency

A Relationship Rescue for Toxic Relationships, Manipulation & Enabling to Self Confidence, Boundaries, Emotional Health & Happiness

Jessica Minty

Table Of Contents

Introduction

I want to sincerely thank you and congratulate you for purchasing my book.

Making the choice to download this book demonstrates a willingness to change. Your simple decision to take action communicates your desire to step out of the shadows and pursue a different way of life. Your choice to change takes bravery, energy and commitment. The only way to truly succeed is by choosing to take one step at a time. Welcome to your first step! You are well on your way.

This straightforward book contains techniques and strategies on how to overcome and recover from codependency. *"Codependency"* will teach you what signs to look for in order to determine if you are in a codependent relationship. At the heart of the book, you will learn how to make changes with your attitudes, thoughts and actions in order to receive freedom from codependency. By the time you are finished with this book, you will be empowered to make drastic changes in your relationships to become codependent no more.

I've witnessed the dynamics of codependency in the lives of others. I've seen people struggle and feel trapped in their codependent relationships, whether they are relationships with other people, food, drugs or alcohol. Their codependent relationship of choice consumes and debilitates that person's life.

Fortunately, I have also seen people free from their codependent relationships. For some people, that may mean ending a relationship. For other people, it may mean changing aspects of their thoughts, feelings or behaviors. As a note: it's important to recognize that freedom from codependency doesn't always have to result in "breaking up" with a person or leaving a marriage. Ideally, that choice should be the last possible option that is accompanied with a lot of serious consideration and counsel from others.

I, too, have experienced the effects of codependency in my own life. It has only been within the last couple years that I discovered what codependency was and realized that I had the tendencies to be codependent. Through reaching out to people, education and practical application, I have been able to obtain my own freedom from codependency with the most important relationships in my life.

I want to thank you again for purchasing *"Codependency."* It truly brings me great joy to see other people seeking solutions and freedom. My desire is for this book to bring encouragement, hope and victory into your own life. Keep seeking, keep looking, keep fighting for your right to joy. I sincerely hope you enjoy the book and find what you're looking for.

Please take some time to stop by and LIKE our Facebook page:

https://www.facebook.com/joypublishing

Sincerely,

Jessica Minty

Chapter 1 – What is Codependency?

Most people are not aware that codependence is an addiction. In fact, it is the most common of all the types of addictions; it is the addiction of looking elsewhere to find happiness and fulfillment. Instead of finding it inside yourself, you try to find your happiness in people and in things that you might lose, like places, experiences, behaviors, things and relationships.

Essentially, your life is defined by that relationship. You are addicted to that relationship. Your behavior, thoughts, and emotions become intertwined with another in an unbalanced manner. You lessen yourself and place the relationship on a pedestal above you. You will do whatever it takes to keep that relationship happy and healthy. Codependency deceives you into thinking that you can control your interior feelings by controlling exterior sources in the form of people, feelings or things. At the core of codependency is control or the lack of control in a person's life.

Unknowingly, people who are codependent put a label on themselves, and labels will never empower you. Labels have become acceptable in today's society as codependency becomes almost synonymous with romance and relationships. However, codependency can often be confused with sacrificial love or martyrdom. But isn't that what love is all about? Giving yourself completely and wholly towards another? Unfortunately, people who are in codependent relationships may not be aware that they are in relationships characterized as such. It is both hard to recognize and hard to end.

Codependent Patterns

It is important to recognize the patterns characteristic of a codependent person. These attributes may snap you out of denial if you didn't think you had codependent tendencies up until this point. Or you'll realize your areas of weakness where attention needs to be given.

As a codependent, you:
- Assume responsibility for others' feelings and behaviors
- Feel guilty about other's feelings and behaviors
- Have difficulty identifying what you are feeling or difficulty expressing feelings
- Are afraid of your own anger, yet sometimes erupt in rage
- Worry about how others may respond to your feelings, opinions, and behavior
- Have difficulty making decisions
- Are afraid of being hurt and/or rejected by others
- Minimize, alter or deny how you truly feel
- Are very sensitive to how others are feeling and feel the same
- Are afraid to express differing opinions or feelings
- Value others opinions and feelings more than your own
- Embarrassed to receive recognition and praise, or gifts
- Judge everything you think, say, or do harshly, as never "good enough"
- Are a perfectionist
- Are extremely loyal, remaining in harmful situations too long
- Do not ask others to meet your needs or desires
- Do not perceive yourself as lovable and worthwhile
- Compromise your own values and integrity to avoid rejection or others' anger

6

(Taken from a Celebrate Recovery resource: "Codependency – The Problem and Solution for Women")

Do you recognize some of these patterns in yourself? You may have one or many. You may be relieved or overwhelmed. Take heart, you are not alone. Keep in mind that people fall on a continuum. Some people can have codependent tendencies that only surface in a particular circumstance with a particular person. Others are engrossed in codependency and can't even leave the house to put gas in their car. While there are always extremes, a majority of the population falls in the middle. Everybody, to some extent, and at some point in their life, will exhibit codependent tendencies in some form or another.

Hopefully, you have been able to identify your own codependent patterns that you can start bringing healing to. It is not until the darkness has been brought to the light does the healing begin. Knowledge of where you stand with codependency is powerful. You have a clear picture of the enemy you are trying to slay. You have clarity and a target to set your focus upon. You are that much closer to victory.

Chapter 2 – Codependent Relationships

When you are in a codependent relationship, you believe in the illusion that your other half holds the key to your own happiness, so when they leave you, they take that happiness with them. In other words, your world comes crashing down. This predisposition is very typical of women with low self esteem. These women wrap their lives around their dating relationship seeking security and significance. Their pattern of thinking becomes very "all or nothing": either their life is consumed by the presence of their partner, or they fall apart when the relationship ends. They become addicted to the person and the feelings entangled in that relationship.

The problem with this illusion is when you fail to realize that you, alone, hold the key to your happiness; it cannot be found in other people, in places, or in things that you continuously cling to. Nothing and nobody will ever be able to make you happy. Things come and go; they break; they get lost; they get stolen. How often do we pursue "things" to only find out that they don't fulfill us in the end? They aren't capable of making us happy. They are just lifeless "things" - nothing more, nothing less. Relationships, on the other hand, are more complex. They have life; they are abstract; they are reciprocal in nature. But people let us down. At some point in time, people will fail us. They'll fall short in some way or another and make mistakes that hurt. This is human nature.

Hidden within relationships is a misconception very commonly believed in modern society. When we are in a relationship, we get this romantic idea that we need to sacrifice ourselves completely for the other person. Women are particularly apt at this. The codependent person lays down their life at the cost of pleasing the other person. Keep in mind that the other person can be a spouse, friend, parent, sibling, child, coworker, etc. The other person's needs are held in high esteem and the codependent person sacrifices themselves in order to meet those needs above their own. This sounds very noble, doesn't it? Isn't this what it looks like to be unselfish...to care for others before yourself? But this is when it gets tricky.

While it is important to love others unselfishly, it is crucial to find a balance. When we compromise our needs and martyr ourselves to the point of depleting ourselves and neglecting our needs, we become out of balance. We need to check our motives. Are our motives driven by guilt, shame, people pleasing, or fear? Then perhaps we aren't really acting out of a motive of unselfish love.

Recognizing a Codependent Relationship

Codependent relationships are in virtually every relationship; it's just that most couples don't recognize the signs or they just ignore these completely. Are you in a codependent relationship? See if these signs are present:

1. You feel that you cannot live without the other person. You are certain that you cannot go on if they leave you.

2. You believe that you need your better half to be happy. You are convinced that no other person can make you happy other than your partner. While other people, like your

family and friends, do make you happy, you are convinced that if you lose your other half, you will stop being happy.

3. You feel trapped. You believe that if you do something drastic, like relocate, change, or simply grow, you will never be happy because you will be abandoning them.

4. You feel intense guilt just thinking of moving away from your partner. Because of the things that they have done for you, you believe that they won't be able to survive if you went away; which is a rather ironic way of reasoning.

5. You feel like you are responsible for saving the other person. This is like the savior syndrome, wherein you are certain that there is no other person who can love and understand them besides you. However, the other person might not like the idea of you saving him or resents you for trying to "save" him.

6. Even if your partner mistreats you, you still tolerate your partner's actions out of love. You are certain that you can weather this so you just continue to tolerate the way they treat you.

7. You believe that if you hold on long enough, your partner will change their ways and finally realize that you don't deserve any of the mistreatments.

8. You feel that there is no way that you can stop the other person from hurting you. You believe that this is your destiny. You are the one who makes excuses for their actions. You believe that you deserve being mistreated and that the only way to prove your love for the other person is to put up with it.

9. You feel that there is no way out of the relationship. You are convinced that if you leave, the other person will never let you and that they will follow you around just so you can take them back. You end up staying in the relationship and continue enduring the abuses and mistreatments.

10. You love and hate the other person with almost the same intensity. You believe that the good times that you had will make the bad times seem trivial and easily forgettable. Unfortunately, that will never happen.

Codependent people tend to deny themselves at any cost in order to make the other person happy or to keep the peace. The root of this behavior is low self esteem. The codependent excessively complies because they don't believe that their needs are worth it. In essence, they teach the other person to treat them like a door mat. Codependent people are easily taken advantage of because they don't stand up for their rights or put their foot down.

Chapter 3 – Why People Become Codependent

Codependency is the product of being exposed to dysfunctional beliefs about relationships and romance. Why do you stay in an abusive relationship? How could you believe that your partner who abuses you still holds the key to your happiness? Why can't you just pack up and leave?

Family Role Models

It all starts during childhood. If you grew up in a home that taught you not to reveal your true feelings and that you should just keep these to yourself, you are likely to develop codependency. It is also possible that you don't have a good relationship model to refer to. You might have witnessed this kind of relationship with your parents or with your friends or other relatives. Thus, you assume that this is the best relationship you can ever get and that if you continue to hold on, everything will eventually turn out fine.

People can often choose partners that mimic characteristics and dynamics of their mother and father relationship. It isn't unusual for a codependent person to marry or partner with someone who is controlling or dominating in some way. You might have seen your parents' abusive relationship. You might have witnessed how your mother stayed in and endured an abusive relationship with your father. You might have heard from your mom that she stayed because she was hoping that your dad would change. She can't leave him because she loves him and she can't let him destroy his life. These thoughts stayed with you and you believed that if you were to end up in the same situation, you would do what your mom did.

Codependency can also be the by-product of parents with extremely high expectations of their children. The result is a child that tries to earn love and people please. Nothing they do can ever feel good enough. They have this never ending drive to obtain their parent's approval. Unfortunately, they may never achieve this heart's desire. There are many stories of individuals that toil in their careers or personal lives in order to attain great success. Their sole purpose is to finally please their demanding parent and hear the words, "Well done" or "I'm proud of you." However, too many times these individuals reach the top only to be disappointed when they don't hear the words the so longed for. Their efforts were in vain because they fixed their eyes on the wrong prize. Rather than trying to chase after folly, we need to seek success for our own joy and fulfillment. We may never get the pat on the back that we hoped for, but in the end, we can be proud of our own efforts. This is true security and happiness.

Others Determine Your Personal Happiness

One of the reasons that you continuously opt to stay in an abusive relationship is that you believe that you cannot find your happiness without the other person. You believe that living alone is worse than being with your partner. You are convinced that if you live alone, away from your partner, you will never find happiness because you have convinced your subconscious mind that you need the other person to be happy and fulfilled.

Ultimately, only you can make yourself happy. You are the one who chooses to be happy, angry, sad, whatever. It's all a matter of perception. With the proper tools and practice, your emotions can be changed instantly. Realistically, at the end of the day, you are responsible for your own happiness. No one else can do it for you.

Fostering the belief that living alone is worse than being with your partner is your own doing. It is a wrong belief that you picked up somewhere along the way. You can continue believing this message and be miserable. Or, you can debunk this limiting belief and create a new truth that brings happiness. The truth of the matter is: the world would not end if you lived alone, away from your partner. It may be unbearable for a time, but in the end, you'd be okay. If you can imagine the worst case scenario, you'll realize that you actually have what it takes to make it through. So what's the new truth from your old limiting belief? The truth is that you can find happiness with or without the other person. In fact, sometimes you may be even happier without the other person – if you can believe it!

Low Self-Esteem

Lack of self-esteem is also one of the causes of codependency. You believe that you deserve this relationship because of who you are. You don't see yourself being able to find a more fulfilling relationship because you feel you are not worthy enough. You are convinced that you are fortunate because your current partner loved you even if you are not worthy. So, even if you hurt, you continue to stay. Low self-esteem causes you to not stand up for yourself; to not speak up when you don't agree; to sweep things

15

under the rug in order to maintain peace; to put other people's needs above your own even at your expense.

There is a deep desire to be needed. You believe that the only way you can regain your self-esteem is to feel needed by your partner. You feel good and you feel fulfilled if your partner depends on you. Typically, people who did not receive unconditional love from their parents while growing up can struggle with feelings of low self-esteem.

A codependent person will do everything to make excuses for whatever wrongdoings other people are doing because that is the only time that they feel needed; it is the "savior" or "caretaker" attitude that is present in most codependent individuals.

An Unhealthy Relationship

A codependent relationship is an unhealthy relationship. You will never get true happiness and fulfillment, which are the very things that you have always wanted to have. If you are a codependent partner, you might be struggling with the fear of being rejected and being abandoned. You long for approval, validation, and appreciation. You feel that you are responsible for your partner to the point of setting aside your own needs and wants; the other person always comes first, even if it means that you have to suffer or go without.

You tend to bury the real problems that are causing the codependency. This behavior doesn't solve the problems; on the contrary, the problems will persist as new ones come in. It will not

16

come as a surprise if you find drug abuse and alcohol abuse in a codependent relationship. The addicted person can often take advantage of the codependent person because they are easily manipulated and controlled. The codependent person will happily oblige in order to keep the peace and not rock the boat. This can create a vicious cycle that very quickly traps the codependent person.

.

Chapter 4 – Codependents and their Personalities

Codependents have a lot to work on regarding their personalities. They are unique individuals on their own, but as codependents they have a lot within them and a lot to learn. They are a work in progress; they have such fragile personalities that hoping to change them will require patience and perseverance.

Codependents as Dependent Personalities

The irony about codependents is that as much as they feel responsible for others and attend to other people, they believe underneath that other people are actually responsible for them. They blame others for their problems and unhappiness, and for them, it's the fault of other people why they are unhappy.

Codependents find it hard to function independently; they must be involved in supportive relationships so they can manage their lives. To maintain their relationships, they will avoid getting angry. They'll become meek and docile; they tend to admire and love endlessly, and will be willing to offer all they can. They seem to be "perfect lovers" – unquestioning, loyal and affectionate, and even considerate and tender on those people whom they rely on.

Unfortunately, these people aren't perfect after all: they feel inferior, and will meet even those unreasonable demands to avoid abandonment and isolation. They'll perhaps resort to abuse and intimidation because they fear they can't function by themselves. Unpleasant tasks are not a problem if it will mean having on hand the support and the care they need. Bonds are important to them, and if various sacrifices have to be made, then so be it.

Getting Better

Yes, you, as a codependent, can get better. How? This is by accepting that success and happiness can only be achieved by changing yourself and not the behavior of other people.

You have to detach yourself from other people and their problems. You have to learn how to stop reacting instinctively and impulsively as rescuers. Be in control of your own life. Getting involved with someone means that s/he will be an addition to your life – not someone who replaces it.

Detachment from Triggers

Detachment should be done emotionally, mentally, and – if necessary – physically from painful and unhealthy relationships. You have to learn how to let go of other people's lives and responsibilities, as well as those problems that you can't solve. By doing so, you'll become the person that you really are, and you'll grow. You'll understand that you can't change others, but you can make your life better.

Getting detached from other people doesn't always indicate that the relationship has to end. Sometimes all you need is *physical detachment*, and you simply have to be away for a while so these people won't provoke you and make you react. Yes, you react because these people are important to you, but you have to realize you can't control these people.

Once you realize that reality isn't all 'sunshine and roses', that's when everything will be clear. You have to admit that you can't fix everything. You can't mold someone into your ideals. You can't force someone to be a person s/he's not.

Going through the Grief Process

Without accepting reality, you can't take that first step to change. However, once you grasp the truth, though, that's when you make things better for yourself. It won't be easy; you'll undergo the grief process.

- Denial – Here you are still in the state of shock. You panic. You're numb. You refuse to acknowledge the situation you are currently in. You are anxious and repress your feelings.

- Anger – You're angry about everything. You're in a stage where you lash out and blame everything and everyone, regardless if justified or not.

- Bargaining – This is the "if... then" stage. You've calmed down by this time, and hope to stop or fix the current situation. You'll say, "If you do this, or I'll do that, then it will be okay."

- Depression – Bargaining and pleading won't work, hence you'll feel sadness and sorrow. You should be with people who'll support you when necessary.

- Acceptance – After you go through the first four steps, then you're on your way to acceptance. Reaching this point doesn't always mean that you're happy, this only means you are at peace with where you are. You understand that you can choose whether to stay or to go on, and you can make the necessary decisions. You have conceded, and are fine with your current situation. You realize that all is well and you've learned from your experiences.

Life is filled with mistakes, and this is inevitable as you learn to take care of yourself. You have to bear in mind that having done wrongs is okay, as long as you know that you were doing the best you could.

In getting better, focus on your goal rather than the recovery process. You have to make sure that the commitment is there to change yourself. Attainable goals are easier to fulfill. With these goals, you'll realize that you can still go on and make a complete recovery as self-reliant, independent and happier individuals.

Chapter 5 – Codependency and Families

Codependency is a developed behavior that can be handed down through generations. It is a behavioral and an emotional condition that influences an individual's capacity to have a mutually, healthy satisfying relationship.

It is also referred to as "relationship addiction" – people with codependency often develop or sustain relationships that tend to be one-sided, emotionally damaging and/or offensive. They hold an exaggerated impression of responsibility for others as well as struggle with setting healthy boundaries. Consequently, they find relationships demanding and often endure from anxiety, guilt, depression, and resentment.

Codependency makes individuals lose themselves while being involved in a relationship. This dysfunction causes them to ignore their needs, feelings and problems while dwelling on others' needs, feelings and troubles. This is known by observing and emulating other family members who show this kind of behavior.

Previously, codependency was a term used for partners that are influenced by chemical dependency, or those people who are living with, or even those involved in a relationship with an addicted person. Recently, however, it has been observed that codependent people either came from, or be a part of dysfunctional families.

Dysfunctional Families and Codependency

Painful circumstances – or parents themselves – can bring anarchy or shock to a family. As an effect, the children are often obliged to forget their childhood and enter survival mode instead. Children in survival mode become hyper vigilant; they tend to scrutinize their surroundings in order to sense any danger to their safety and well-being.

Children like these quickly learn to disregard their needs and feelings – they feel incapable to modify their conditions and/or have caretakers who are too overwhelmed to provide the foundation they absolutely need. Or, worse, they fear of being reprimanded for expressing their emotions and needs. In effect, they deny introspection as a risky luxury that might get in the way with alertness for the next threat.

Eventually, these children become skilled in disconnecting from their feelings and needs and, instead, develop defensive strategies of trying to have reign over others for safety, and to obtain the love and acceptance they long for.

Different Kinds of Families

Today's family life shows various types of family paradigms common in society. Here are different kinds of families, and how one can be distinguished from the others.

Functional Families

Functional families are what most people desire to have. This type of family has open communication lines between the children and their parents. Children are allowed to provide their inputs into family matters, but it's still the parents who make the final verdict with regard to the child's wellbeing.

A family unit like this is distinguished through a sense of family in its entirety. Every family member feels the sense of belonging that adds to their high self-esteem. The family trusts their children and they feel comfortable enough to invite their kids' friends into their homes.

In a nurturing family, it's okay to have feelings... and to discuss them. Individual differences are acknowledged, and people offer respectful criticism to come with proper consequences for actions. The household has a relaxed and joyful atmosphere.

Dysfunctional Families

People growing up in dysfunctional families experience pain and trauma from their parents' words, actions and attitudes. This trauma causes them to grow up differently from other children, and miss out on other important parts of parenting that get them ready for adulthood.

People instinctively protect their inner feelings, and they tend to have low self-worth. They also try to avoid – and even deny –

stress; they feel hurt, tired, and disappointed. They suffer from anger, fear, shame or pain usually denied or ignored.

Family members value performance more than the person, yet there's still a great deal of control and criticism. There are many taboo subjects and secrets that should not be discussed, and everybody must obey the rules of the strongest person's thoughts and standards. The atmosphere is tense, and you can feel anger and fear everywhere. There is shaming and punishment, and the policies are inconsistent, unclear, and rigid.

How Parents Can Prevent Codependency

Children build their own identity and how to value, recognize and convey needs and feelings through exchanges with their parents. The parents' manner of communicating with your children is vital to the foundation of their individuality and to a large extent confirms how stable the child's gist of self and self-esteem are.

As parents, there are seven major things they can do to make sure their children grow up and develop into independent adults:

1. Agree to freedom of information.

One of the key characteristics of functional families and associations, even countries, is freedom to state ideas and opinions. Secrets and no-talk policies are frequently observed in dysfunctional families. Instances such as not allowing them to mention grandma's limp or daddy's drinking habits teaches children to be frightened and to have reservations on their perceptions and themselves. Children are naturally inquisitive about everything. This is healthy and should be encouraged, not squelched.

2. Acknowledge your children's feelings and thoughts.

Children complain about not being allowed to express anger, complain, be sad, or even become excited. They teach themselves to contain their feelings. This becomes challenging towards their adult relationships and can eventually become depression. Giving children a chance to let their feelings out produces a healthy outlet.

Feelings don't need to be rational, and you're not forced to "fix" them. You can comfort your children instead; you should also let them know you love and care for them, rather than attempting to talk them out of how they feel.

3. Take care of your children.

Parents can't give their children too much love and understanding. This isn't actually spoiling them. Some parents use presents or not setting boundaries to express their love, but this isn't a replacement for affection and empathy, which children need to develop into self-assured, loving adults.

4. Show respect to your children.

When you show respect, this means you listen and take them seriously. By doing so, you make them understand that who they are, what they think and what they feel have worth and merit.

You don't necessarily have to say yes with what they say, but listening to understand indicates that you respect them, hence teaching them self-respect. Talk to your children with courtesy. Criticizing tones should be avoided as this destroys your child's self-esteem; instead, praise the behavior you desire. Setting boundaries and explain negative consequences of behavior you want dislike without name-calling or criticizing can be possible.

Treating your child with respect will make him treat others with respect as well; he'll also expect the same in future relationships.

5. Show consideration for your children's limits.

Respecting children's thoughts and feelings indicate that you respect their boundaries. Verbal abuse and harmful actions violate their boundaries, and unwanted touch and sexual exposure or intimacy will make them uncomfortable. Tickling beyond a child's comfort level is included as well. Additionally, children's space, property, and privacy should be honored. Reading their letters or journals, or even talking to their friends behind their back are unacceptable behaviors.

6. Have predictable, reasonable, humane policies and penalties.

Codependents grow up in families where there are no policies or the rules are cruel and rigid, or conflicting and subjective. Children need a safe, predictable, and just environment. When rules and punishments seem unfair, instead of realizing faults and mistakes, the children become anxious and angry, and tend to distrust other people including their parents and people with authority.

Rules should be clear and consistent; parents have to be united. The priority should be what's important and what is reasonably enforceable instead of having your focus on regulations and penalties in the moment. State the rules to older children, let them raise their questions if any, and have good reasons to support your decisions.

7. Allow children to come up with age-appropriate decisions, to be responsible and to be independent.

Children need assistance in solving problems and making decisions. They also need to take on responsibilities even at a young age, and not to take anything or to rely on anybody. Children are different: some are controlled, some are pampered. Some become dependent and get scared of deciding for themselves, and others are not guided properly with unlimited freedom.

Children defy control because they look for self-control. They by nature push for independence. This isn't rebelliousness; encourage this behavior as long as you set age-appropriate limits. Once they're ready to test their wings, give them guidance to help them out in making their own decisions as well as the freedom to commit and learn from their mistakes.

Parents play a major part in making sure that their children grow up to become healthy individuals. If the parents themselves don't function properly as good role models, then the children will be affected in major ways that will influence their lives and their way of thinking until they become adults and start their own families.

Chapter 6 – Codependency and Boundaries

Codependency actually comes from a lack of boundaries. All the scenarios and symptoms of a codependent relationship lead back to the lack of mental, psychological, emotional, and physical boundaries of an individual. As mentioned in the previous chapter, it originated from the family and how that individual was raised.

It comes from believing that there is a need for you to be connected to a dysfunctional person who mistreats you. It is also rooted in the premise that you cannot set a boundary because if you did, you can kiss your happiness goodbye.

You have to connect with your anger in order to get out of that codependent relationship. Why? Because anger is the universe's signal that a boundary has been violated. Listen to your anger and constructively work with it; then you can begin setting the boundaries so you can work on building healthy relationships.

A healthy relationship is one in which the two individuals have healthy personal boundaries. In the absence of personal boundaries, a codependent relationship exists. On the other hand, when there are strong and healthy boundaries, there exists an interdependent relationship.

However, defining boundaries and getting in touch with your anger are just the initial steps of overcoming a codependent relationship. Don't be surprised when the other person reacts to the boundaries you are setting. They aren't accustomed to you behaving in this way. They are used to a particular demeanor from you. They may push back, get angry or behave poorly as a result. None the less, don't waiver in setting your boundaries. Keep firm and continue being firm. Over time, they will learn that this is the new you and adjust themselves accordingly.

Setting Healthy Boundaries

Boundaries contribute to your growth as well as your sense of self. Taking risks and learning about true identities make your boundaries emerge, thus taking you to your higher being. Balance in life is good – it helps you develop a healthy being and understand how others should treat you.

There's nothing wrong with giving so long as you don't allow others to "invade your territory" and rob you. Healthy boundaries give you power, make you stronger, and provide you courage to stand manipulation.

How can you set boundaries?

Forget anger. Don't set boundaries when you are angry. When filled with anger, you tend to use lengthy arguments and are likely to attack the other person. It's best to communicate using a few words and by being specific. Sometimes anger is necessary when setting boundaries, but resentment should not be involved in setting one.

Your boundaries must match your behavior. Congruity is another vital prerequisite in establishing your boundaries. If your attitude does not match the boundaries you're trying to set, then your plans won't work. When setting boundaries, don't apologize and don't rationalize. Don't be neither scared nor ashamed, and listen to yourself.

Prepare for consequences... and enforce them if necessary. To set boundaries, you also have to have a particular type of readiness. You won't be able to enforce these boundaries if you're not ready for them. Your readiness is connected to your insight and personal growth; once you realize it's much needed – you can't tolerate others' attitude towards you anymore – that's when you can enforce it.

Take care of your needs. Ask yourself: what are those that you like and don't like? What brings you pleasure? Once you find the answers, you can get engaged in self-nurturing activities, and you won't get guilty in doing so. After all, you're simply taking care of yourself. You'll enjoy life more once you're able to set a healthy boundary.

To End or Not to End?

If you ever come to the conclusion that you need to end your codependent relationship, tread carefully. This is a decision not to be taken lightly. Ending a codependent relationship can be tricky. When you try to end it, you should make sure that you still break it off in a healthy way; otherwise, it could be the source of more problems. This is because you might end up setting the boundaries out of fear. You cannot stick around after you have set boundaries out of fear and expect the relationship to last. Most of the time, relationships based on fear are unhealthy and the dissolution of such relationships could come in just a matter of time.

Ending a relationship with a codependent using the wrong methods isn't healthy; doing so may commit more harm than good. If you won't do the process correctly, you end up setting a boundary that's fueled by fear. Fear-based decisions rarely end up as beneficial ones. Boundaries set because of fear won't work, and you shouldn't expect them to last. They're neither well-reasoned nor sensible as well, and won't emerge as constructive for you and your partner.

How Not to End a Codependent Relationship

- Playing the blaming-game before ending the relationship

- Dumping the other person without giving a reason why

- Ending the relationship without warning

- Hurting them on purpose as you end it

- Sugar-coating the break-up piece so as not to hurt the other person

- Getting someone else to do it for you

- Abruptly running away

- Leading the person on – giving them the illusion that this is not the end and there is hope for a relationship in the future

Chapter 7 – Caregiving vs. Caretaking

People usually consider themselves as caring people. They express the care through actions. There is, however, a little known and darker side to this act of caring for other people and which is neither talked about enough nor well fathomed.

One behavior associated with codependency is caretaking – which is not ideal – and should be replaced by caregiving. Codependency causes you to have unhealthy relationships, and caretaking is one of those qualities that should not be exercised.

Differences between Caregiving and Caretaking

There are vital differences between caregiving and caretaking. In a healthy relationship, the happier and healthier you both are, the more you do caregiving rather than caretaking. Caretaking is a dysfunctional behavior that can still be changed. It should be lessened, or better yet, eliminated if possible. Your objective is to do as much caregiving and as less caretaking as you can – in order to experience more contentment, peace and happiness in your relationships.

Caregiving

When someone needs care and assistance, whether caused by a chemical dependency, chronic medical state, or being cured from any illness, the one who provides the nurturing is called the caregiver. The caregiver is possibly a friend, family member, or health professional. This person gives support and comfort to another when necessary. The assistance is provided with kindness and compassion, emerging from a place filled with love and without any expectations of receiving something as payment. Caregivers can rely on and acknowledge the patient's position on his or her chosen path and will not meddle nor try to change it.

Caretaking

A caretaker also extends a helping hand when needed. He can be a friend, family member, or professional. This person gives what he or she thinks as comfort and support, and usually waits for something in return -- he "gives to get". A caretaker may attempt to modify the outcome and not allow the patient's path take its natural course. Through a caretaker's eyes, what he or she does is out of love; however, there is possibly a subconscious or underlying motive of fear.

Here are other ways on how you can distinguish caregiving from caretaking:

Caretaking

- Worry
- Crosses boundaries
- Think they understand what's best for other people
- Immediately rush into action when a problem comes up
- Consider self-care as a selfish act, and therefore avoids it
- Usually attracts needy people
- Focuses on the problem
- Uses "you" a lot

Caregiving

- Solve problems and take action
- Respects boundaries
- Only know what's good for themselves
- Wait to be asked for help before taking action
- Practice self-care to take care of others
- Usually attracts healthy people
- Focuses on the solution
- Uses "I" more

You cross the line between caregiving and caretaking when your personal energy is channeled to others who are perfectly able of taking care of themselves. This is usually triggered by caring too much, or the choice of doing more than you should as caring, when in fact, it is already caretaking.

What makes caretaking so hard to detect by the untrained eye to spot is about the actions of the person being camouflaged under the idea of caring. More often than not, the person who's also a caretaker is unaware of what they are doing simply because it feels a lot like love and intimacy although it's actually not.

Of course you always want to have a smooth flowing relationship. No one wants to be with someone who's unhappy all the time. You care and provide all the attention that you can shower to your partner. But how do you know if it's no longer "caring", but instead being "codependent"?

Problems start to arise when helping starts to feel hurting; you feel fear, and this is where your relationship is based on. Clearly, this isn't good, as this ends up not being healthy for everyone involved. Simply put, caretaking starts from insecurity. It's a codependency hallmark wherein you are in a need to be in control. Caregiving, on the other hand, is an illustration of love and kindness.

For a caretaker, it can be quite a revelation to realize that it's better to be liked and appreciated for who you are, instead of being liked and appreciated just because you gave someone what he or she needed at that time. Being with someone doesn't have to come with reasons or conditions.

Chapter 8 – Practical Solutions for Codependent Tendencies

Identifying a codependent relationship is tricky. It is often disguised in any individual's willingness to adapt to other people's needs.

People in general consciously or unconsciously assign all the people in their lives a role to assume. They then deal with these people based on what they think these people want from them. In essence, it's like presenting a puppet show of your life. You may not realize it, but you are orchestrating the whole show based on what you conceptualize in your head.

There are people who are somewhat oblivious of the "roles" they assume, some seem to be detached, and others run along the lines of being codependent. In order to put an end to or overcome a codependent relationship, you need to recognize a person who "suffers" from codependency.

You will find in the succeeding paragraphs some of the most common codependent "roles." Do not be surprised if you recognized yourself in more than one. In addition, you will find some strategies on how you can change the script so nobody becomes the codependent party.

1. Martyr

For martyrs, suffering is virtuous. They are happy when they were able to put the needs of their loved ones ahead of their own. They are the ones who would be the first one to take on an extra project and always the last person to leave the office. They would pick up the tab voluntarily even if they are broke. Recognize the signs? It might have been the concept that your parents and your religious belief has instilled in you.

The Issue: You might not have realized it yet, but when sacrifice is your norm when it comes to relationships with loved ones, friends, and colleagues, you tend to neglect your own needs to be loved and cared for. While these are the things that you are hoping to get by giving more than you can give, chances are your efforts can backfire. When you don't get what you want from the relationship, you'll begin to resent these very same people to whom you've extended your help.

How to Overcome: Begin to care for yourself

It is important that you understand the difference between self-care and selfishness. You have to realize that you are not being selfish if you opt to leave the office on time or if you want to go out with friends once in a while. Also, it isn't rude if you ask to split the bill if you can't afford to shoulder everything. You have to begin to care for yourself because no one else will. Ernest Hemingway, an American author and journalist, once said, "My health is the main capital I have and I want to administer it intelligently." If we don't have our health, we have nothing left to give. It's similar to the idea of how to respond to an emergency in a plane crash: put on your oxygen mask first before helping others or else you are no help to either of you.

2. Savior

A savior takes pride in being the one to solve all conflicts. He is the one who's always there to lend money when a friend needs it, even if he is equally broke.

The Issue: There is no denying that everyone does need help sometimes and it is not bad to help. However, if you feel it is your personal mission to be the one to give comfort to others, even to the point of creating discomfort on your part, it is not healthy. You are telling the people you've helped that they are hopeless without you. You teach them to become overly dependent on you. As a result, you've created a relational dynamic that will continuously suck energy, time and resources out of you. People can learn to take advantage of this. They can even manipulate you to get what they want. When people get used to you being their savior, they quickly react when you don't perform that role in their life.

How to Overcome: Empower

It is always a good thing to help; it's a win-win situation because you feel good when you are able to be of help. However, you have to examine your real purpose for helping other people. It is also important to analyze if it is also doing them good. Being there for them is one thing but preventing them from being self-reliant is another. There are people whom you have helped once who come in for another and then another until they are totally dependent on you that they do nothing to improve their own situation. It's not rude to occasionally say "no." When you save people from their problems, you may actually be robbing them of a lesson that they need to learn for themselves. If you feel that helping other people is the only time that you are needed and loved, then you are not in a healthy relationship at all.

3. Adviser

Are you an adviser? You probably have an ability to look into someone else's problems and offer solutions and advice. The adviser is not too good a listener, though.

The Issue: People come to you because you give good advice. You feel happy because they constantly come to you to hear what you have to say. You assume that they lack self-esteem to even solve their own problems. In reality, though, advisers are the ones who are really insecure and they feel needed when people come to them. They are the ones who lack self-esteem. They want to feel in charge and in control and the only way they can do that is to tell someone what they have to do.

How to Overcome: Set boundaries

If someone comes to you and pours their heart out, try to listen to them for a change. Just by listening, you are able to help your friend or your loved one. You don't have to tell them what to do. Let them make the decision themselves. Let them see for themselves the perfect solution to their problems. You can give them your two cents' worth but only after you have listened to them, and do not tell them what to do. Give them options and then let them decide. Do not tell them outright that they have to do this or that. Respect their own judgment; be a friend and just listen. Ultimately, people need to come to their own conclusions about their problems.

4. People Pleaser

The people pleaser is the one who always volunteers to organize something for the community. They are the ones who volunteer to fix everything. They bask in the glory of being "appreciated" for their hard work in initiating gatherings, parties, and fund drives.

The Issue: It is not really a problem if you are the go-to person when it comes to social gatherings, but it becomes a problem when you begin to feel that doing so becomes a chore yet you cannot say "no" because you don't want them to stop liking you. People-pleasing is passive manipulation. You do things for other people because you can get something from them.

How to Overcome: Learn to Say No

It is not your loss if you say "no." The next time the office needs a volunteer, think twice before stepping up to do the task. Analyze if people are indeed going to dislike you if you didn't volunteer. Are you up for another task? Don't you have other important things to do at home? Learn to say "no" not because you don't want to do it but because there are other more important things that you need to do. There is always a time for everything. Besides, the world won't fall apart if you say "no." You can be replaced. People are capable of finding other people to help.

5. The Person who Says "Yes" All the Time

Have you ever been in a situation when you had to say "yes" when you really wanted to say "no?" Did you resent your action? A person who says "yes" all the time is one who keeps his discomfort to himself.

You can't tell your friends what you really feel for fear of offending them. You can tell your partner that you are upset because you didn't want to start a fight.

The Issue: A healthy relationship is one in which both parties or a group of friends are in total honesty with each other. If you avoid conflicts so you just say "yes" when you meant to say "no," there is a disconnect somewhere in the honesty department there.

In the office, there is something that you are uncomfortable with but you are too afraid to tell your boss for fear that you might lose your job. With your partner, you are afraid to trigger an argument because you fear that they might leave you. So, you hide the feelings inside. When this happens, you might end up resenting them and eventually ruin your relationships.

How to Overcome: Be Honest

If you don't speak up, you will not resolve anything. Your partner might not be aware that there is a problem already until it blows up in your faces. It takes courage to tell the truth but it is liberating. You can tell the truth without hurting someone else's feelings. Talking about a problem doesn't always equate to creating conflicts; this is just the healthier way of bringing up unresolved issues to find solutions.

Did you identify yourself in any of these? You were able to hurdle the first step to making changes in your life: awareness of the "problem." Acceptance that there is a problem is critical in making improvements.

Chapter 9 – Reclaiming Yourself from Codependency

People become codependent longer than they should because they are scared of being alone or feel accountable for their partner's happiness. They may say their desire to break free – but end up staying instead. Others may go away but end up committing the similar self-damaging mistakes once they get in a new relationship. The adrenaline rush felt when they experience passionate feelings toward someone can be captivating. For a lot of people, the rationale behind extreme emotional reliance on a partner is codependency – a tendency to put other's needs before their own.

No matter how hopeless it may appear, codependent people can still break free from their emotional struggles. Regardless of how low they may have felt during their worst moments, they can still recover from this condition.

Raising Your Self-Esteem

Self-esteem is an assessment of someone's worth, or how an individual judges himself. It's also defined as a person's competency in coping with life's basic challenges, and deserving of happiness. Self-esteem one of codependency's main symptoms, and it has to be addressed as soon as possible.

Codependents often have sensitive self-esteem combined with the fear of abandonment or rejection. The "esteem" they have is based on how others see them and perceive their character. They live by solving problems of other people, and this boosts their morale in a distorted way. If something goes awry, they take the blame and bear the guilt. They fill up their schedule to focus on one person – they have this feeling of being needed, and this feeling overcomes everything else.

Codependents usually come from dysfunctional, troubled, or repressed families. They deny it, though, hence the failure of solving their personal issues brought by them being codependents.

They take the blame for almost everything yet also blame others for everything. They reject compliments but are saddened when they don't get complimented. They are scared of being rejected yet reject themselves. They don't think they will be loved or liked, so they tend to show others they are lovable enough to be accepted by other people.

How should you reclaim your self-esteem?

- Challenge any self-defeating thoughts or beliefs about self-worth. You don't have to confirm anything to anyone about yourself.

- See yourself in a loving relationship that fulfills your desires and meets your needs. If your present relationship is damaging, look at ways on how you self-sabotage and observe your own behaviors.

- Tell yourself everyday that it's healthy to receive help from others, and it's an indication of strength rather than weakness. Friendships, counseling, and other online resources can be ultimately helpful to guide you in looking for a happy relationship.

- Become aware of any negative judgments you have about yourself. Don't be harsh; you have to be kind and compassionate on yourself.

- Don't be afraid of rejection; go ahead and get involved in intimate and loving relationships. Concede and let go of your shield, and allow others in your life.

Have you considered that you're just hooked on the pain brought by love? If yes, then remind yourself that you risk your chances of having happy and healthy relationships where your needs can be fulfilled. Are you afraid of being alone? Are you scared of taking a risk? By doing so, you prevent yourself from seeking the happiness and love you deserve.

Focus on your healing and your personal growth – by doing so, you'll begin to transform your life and attract others who are in the same emotional level as you.

Overcoming Guilt and Resentment

Sometimes, guilt is good. Guilt can make people empathize, take the right course of action and to make themselves better individuals. After guilt, forgiveness of oneself should always follow as it's an essential key to life and relationships. For many, however, self-acceptance still remains hard to get hold of due to unhealthy guilt, and this guilt can stay with a person for years, decades, or even for a lifetime.

Guilt is a possible persistent source of pain. You keep on reminding yourself to condemn yourself and to be guilty, and it ends up destroying you and meddling with your goals. Guilt brings anger and resentment, not only to yourself but to people around you.

Why should negative feelings such as guilt, resentment and anger be avoided? One, they absorb your energy. Two, they bring illness and depression. Three, they prevent you from having happiness, success and fulfilled relationships. They hinder you from moving on and stop you from moving forward.

Codependents usually have guilt within them. It's common for them to accept the blame and feel responsible for another's wrongdoings because of their lack of self-esteem. Guilt, however, should be differentiated with shame; shame is when you feel inadequate and inferior, and tends to underestimate yourself and your relationships.

How do you overcome these feelings of shame, guilt and resentment? Ask these questions to yourself, and follow the steps.

- Take responsibility if you've been rationalizing your actions. Tell yourself, "Yes, I did it." Look back and remember what happened. Think about how you felt, and think about other people involved in the process. Consider what were your needs during those times, and if they were met. If those needs weren't met, then why weren't they? What were your motives in doing so? Was there any catalyst for such behavior? Is this catalyst connected to a person or an event in your past? You can write them all down, with a dialogue that includes your feelings.

- While growing up, how were your feelings and mistakes handled? Were you judged for them? Punished? Forgiven? Were people hard on you because of those mistakes? Were you somehow made to feel ashamed?

- How do you judge yourself? Are they really based on your personal faith and principles, or are they based on someone else's approval? Do you still need someone else's support before you go for something that you like? Don't aim to live up on another person's expectations – there are instances on which you'll never get their approval, and in doing so, you might end up sacrificing your own happiness and wants.

- Are your current actions matched with your true values? If not, think of your thoughts, emotions and beliefs that made you do your actions. What may have led you to abandon your values? In violating your values, you end up hurting yourself, which is more painful than hurting someone else.

- How did these conflicts affect you and other people? Take note of those people that you've hurt, and remember that you've hurt yourself as well. Reflect on how you can make amends and ask forgiveness from these people – how can you make things better? Can you still do something to ease the pain?

- If someone did you wrong, you'd possibly forgive them easily. Why then would you treat yourself differently? Do you think it benefits you to punish yourself continually?

- There's nothing wrong with making mistakes as long as you learn from them. Remorse is acceptable – even healthy – and it leads to creating corrective action. You'll learn how to act differently. Write yourself a letter filled with appreciation, understanding and forgiveness. Repeat these words to yourself: *I forgive myself. I'm innocent. I love myself.*

- Surround yourself with people who won't judge you for your past. Share to them what you did. Avoid secrecy to avoid further prolonging guilt and shame.

What is a healthy and humble attitude? You believe you're at fault but you still forgive yourself. Others were wrong, yet you forgive them. You regret the things that happened in the past yet you understand it was just a part of being human, and you ended up learning from your mistakes and you gain experience.

Yes, that is a healthy attitude.

Separating Responsibilities

Another vital task that codependents have to understand is how to separate responsibilities for themselves and for others. They react on other people's concerns. As these problems become more intense, codependents' reactions are more intense as well. They tend to be more involved in the process, hence keeping them in a chaotic state, as well as the people around them. Their energies are focused on other people and their problems which makes them less attentive to their own lives.

In rescuing, codependents aim to take care of people who can perfectly live their own lives. They dwell on problems they don't have control over, and can be upset when things go wrong. What they don't know is that rescuing these people from their responsibilities doesn't help them grow but instead makes them evade the outcome of their actions more. Love makes codependents undertake in manipulative behavior. Their intentions are to help, and they end up being people who force things to happen using too much effort and energy.

Codependents fail to realize that other people don't need controlling, and these people would usually have no interest in obtaining the outcome the Codependent is aiming for. Codependents must understand as well that people will simply do what they wish to do regardless if they're wrong or right, or if they're hurting themselves.

Codependents who do another person's task doesn't help the person be better by rescuing them -- they instead actually teach them to be more dependent, and will lead to them taking advantage of the Codependent. In return, the codependent becomes resentful, overburdened, and ultimately vengeful and upset simply because they do things they don't wish to do.

Chapter 10 – How to Recover from Codependency

Recovery from codependency will need a lot of effort and determination from you. It might require you to make a 180-degree turnaround of the patterns that you have been used to. However, your healing will bring about strong characteristics that you can benefit from:

- You become authentic

- You become independent

- You open yourself to intimacy

- Your values, feelings, thoughts, beliefs, and actions are aligned

In anything, change is difficult but it is good. There is no shortcut to being free from something that you have been accustomed to. Similar to recovery from any addiction, you have to overcome it.

Since change and recovery take time, the following techniques can help you:

- Your main goal is to bring the attention back to yourself. It doesn't mean becoming self-centered that you end up alienating your friends. Practice sobriety. You need the help of other people, and they need your help too, but you have to make sure that you make guided discernment. You can't say "yes" all the time as you cannot save the world. You learn to detach and you stop being too controlling. This way, you begin to become independent and more self-oriented.

- Since codependency is a form of addiction, you need to stop denying and start becoming aware of the real problems. Codependents who are in abusive relationships endure the pain for fear of being alone; little do they know that they are slowly leading their lives into total destruction.

The first step to your recovery from codependency is to recognize that you are in a codependent relationship. Be aware of the signs and indications that you are in such a relationship. Regain your self-esteem by being true to yourself and admitting that there is a problem.

- Recovery involves acceptance. There is no shortcut to your recovery because it takes time and you have to patient. Recovery and healing is a life-long journey that you have to take, but before you can begin changing your life, you have to learn to accept your situation and accept that you need to make some life-changing decisions.

It takes a great level of maturity to learn to accept. When you are able to accept, you will be opening some new doors towards change, fresh ideas, and renewed energy. These are doors you have long ignored because you have been living in a codependent relationship.

Aside from accepting the situation, you also need to accept yourself. Accept that you are not perfect and you have flaws. When you can accept yourself like that, you don't have to do whatever it takes to make people like you. When you emanate self-esteem and renewed confidence in yourself, the right people will be drawn to you. They will be your true friends.

Acceptance teaches you to be more real and assertive. You begin to find out what you really want. You stop being too manipulating and you enjoy your relationships more because of the mutual respect and honest intimacy.

- Act on it. As most people say, insight without action can only get you so far. If you want to grow as a person and improve your life, you have to turn over a new leaf. You can't grow without taking risks. Get out of your comfort zone. Find your voice and use it well. Speak up and say what you want to say. Do not worry about what you will say; if it comes from the heart, it is sincere and true.

- If you have been in an abusive relationship for so long and you have in effect lost your freedom, try something new or go somewhere on your own.

- Do not rely on anybody to make you happy and fulfilled. Find your own happiness and fulfillment. Do the things that you've always wanted to do but you were just too afraid to do.

- Seek support. When you find yourself in a codependent relationship, you'll feel lost and confused at times. It's important to build a support network that you can fall upon in times of need. The wider your net, the better. Incorporate coworkers, friends, family, community resources, Internet forums, etc. People trapped in relationships with addictions can find much comfort from programs such as Al-Anon. Al-Anon is specific to friends and family of problem drinkers. However, there are many other programs that can be found in the community on a variety of different addictions.

- Accept the inevitable: you can't change the other person, you can only change yourself. This truth is at the core of all Al-Anon and other 12 step programs and is not just limited to these addiction recovery programs. It is true for all relationships regardless of how healthy or unhealthy. The Serenity Prayer, a prayer used in Alcoholics Anonymous, has become widely known throughout the North American culture. This prayer is commonly quoted in a variety of different circumstances in order to bring comfort and strength. Perhaps, you too will find comfort and strength from this famous prayer:

    "God, grant me the serenity to accept the things I cannot change, the courage to change the things I can, and wisdom to know the difference" (Reinhold Niebuhr).

When you regain confidence in yourself, you become empowered and more assertive. You begin to say what you really feel without offending other people. While you work on your relationships with other people, you shouldn't lose yourself in the process.

Avoiding a Relapse

When you begin your healing from codependency, you begin to feel your pain. Do not lose that pain, lest you fall back into being codependent. Listen to your pain and what it is telling you. Listen to your anger and know what it wants to convey to you.

You don't get out of a relationship that has hurt you just so you will not be reminded of the pain you had to go through. Even if you get rid of the person, if you don't begin to heal yourself from within, you will always be vulnerable. Work on yourself and everything else will follow.

The Good Side of Codependency

You don't just get out of a codependent relationship by separating from your partner. It doesn't work that way. Instead of getting rid of the person, why not reconnect with yourself first?

Going back, your goal in overcoming a codependent relationship is to find yourself again. It got lost when you focused on pleasing other people so much that you forgot all about it. You can go through the process of healing without isolating yourself from the very people that you love. You just reconnect and reorganize your priorities.

Complete healing means you are able to live beyond the imperfection of your own personality and of humanity as a whole. You begin to see that living in a chaotic and dangerous world makes you vulnerable and you'll find strength in being true to yourself.

This knowledge and acceptance of who you are as a person will make you stronger and let you create more lasting relationships. The trick with relationships is to discover your joy and happiness regardless of the other person's thoughts, feelings and actions. The key is to understand your self worth and set boundaries. This is true freedom from codependency.

Chapter 11 – Mirror Neurons and Codependency

Brain science sheds a whole new light on relationships and the role they play in our life. Only within the last 20ish years has science discovered the marvelous reactions of mirror neurons. They are essentially the mind's mirror. Scientists once believed that people used logical thinking processes to figure out how other people behave. However, mirror neurons reveal that we actually predict and interpret other people's behaviors by feelings.

Up until the 1990s, scientist understood that neurons fire off when a person performs a particular action. However, research is now revealing that mirror neurons fire off when a person simply *observes* another person making the same action. This ability allows us to empathize with other human beings. It means that our brain replicates other people's emotions and intentions behind an action without us actually performing that action.

Using the example of smiling, brain scientists observed the same neurons light up in the brain of the person smiling as the person who witnessed the other person smiling. The effects of smiling that the smiling person would feel are also felt by the person not doing the smiling. This powerful information means that we are way more connected than we ever realized...even in ways that we aren't consciously aware of.

So how does this relate to codependency? Codependency typically has a negative spin to it – it is undesirable to be codependent with another person. Our modern North American culture prizes independency. This value is characteristic of individualistic parenting where a parent trains a child to grow up to care for themselves. However, mirror neurons contradict this belief.

Mirror neurons teach us that we are greatly influenced by the people around us, particularly the ones closest to us. Without our awareness, our brains are continuously incorporating the other people's actions, goals and beliefs. What mirror neurons mean for codependency is that our intimate partners are having a profound influence on our brain without us even knowing it. This is insightful information that explains the reasons why people can be more susceptible to codependency.

In actual reality, humans are hard wired to be in relationship. Over thousands of years, human beings have evolved to fit in, not to stand out. We are genetically built to follow along rather than be individual and separated from others. This is contrary to our North American ideals.

Along with mirror neurons comes another component that influences our brain: complex contagion or social contagion. The counterpart of social contagion is simple contagion. Simple contagion occurs when a disease is spread from one person to another, similar to passing a cold to another person. It's logical to think that when we are in contact with a contagious person, we are at higher risk of contracting that same illness.

Social Contagion

Complex or social contagion is different in the sense that we can pass on "social viruses" by simply being in the presence of another individual. Social viruses can include smoking, drinking, drugs, obesity, depression, loneliness, and happiness. However, do not fear about contracting social viruses. The process doesn't happen that easily. Social contagion isn't as simplistic as merely standing next to a person and contracting their social "disease." Social contagion research is more intricate.

In the Annals of Internal Medicine 152 (2010), J. Niels Rosenquist, MD, PhD, et al, conducted a study to discover the likelihood an individual had of drinking heavily based on their degree of separation to their social network. The study showed that a person was 50% more likely to drink heavily if their best friend drank heavily (1 degree). This likelihood was 36% if a friend of a friend drank heavily (2 degrees). Furthermore, a person had a 16% chance of drinking heavily if a friend of a friend of a friend drank heavily (3 degrees). Lastly, there was a 0% chance with the 4th degree of separation. This research demonstrates that social viruses can be passed along within a social network up to 3 degrees of separation. Can you imagine what this means for people who are codependent?

It's no wonder why people wrestle so much with codependency. We are hard wired to be influenced by the feelings and actions of the ones closest to us: our parents, our partners, our close friends, our coworkers. The information about mirror neurons and social contagion almost seems to set us up for failure. But we can use this information to our advantage. We can start to take control of the people we choose to surround ourselves with.

We can purposely choose to be around people who own the very traits and characteristics we desire. You want to be confident? Hang around confident people. Simply being in their presence means that your brain will begin to adopt their tendencies. The same goes for any other quality you desire: success, joy, self control, weight loss, happiness, etc.

Knowing what we know about mirror neurons and social contagion means that we have to be that much more careful hanging around the people who are closest to us. This doesn't translate to you leaving your partner because they are a negative influence. However, it does add a challenging dimension to your recovery from codependency. What it does translate to is the fact that you can be more compassionate towards yourself when you fall into codependent habits. Remember, we are built to fit in, not stand out. We are meant to be more intertwined than our North American culture allows. Perhaps, in the end, a little bit of dependency isn't such a bad thing when it's in balance with a healthy respect for you.

Conclusion

I would like to thank you once again for purchasing *"Codependency."*

I truly hope this book was able to help you to overcome your codependency tendencies. The next step is to act and make the changes necessary in order to see the real sweetness of freedom.

The journey may be full of ups and downs. Do expect hiccups along the way. Decide on which boundaries you would like to set for yourself and implement them in your relationships. Don't be surprised if people push back or behave negatively when you affirm your boundaries. This is to be expected. They are not used to you having boundaries and it will take time for them to learn how to respect the boundaries you have put in place.

Take care of your self. The core of codependency is low self esteem. The more you believe you are worth it, the more you will stand up for yourself. Continuously remind yourself of your value. Surround yourself with others that will also remind you. The more deeply rooted you are, the less likely you will falter from the storms of other peoples' emotions, behaviors and expectations.

Set your mind and keep it set...you will achieve victory in your life. You deserve it!

I would love for you to share your experiences, stories and encouragements with me. My email address is jessicamintykindle@gmail.com

In addition, please remember to check out our Facebook page in order to find other resources and upcoming promotions:

https://www.facebook.com/joypublishing

Finally, if you enjoyed this book and found it meaningful, please take the time to share your thoughts and post a positive review on Amazon. I greatly appreciate your time and effort.

Deeply grateful,

Jessica Minty

Preview Of "Self Confidence: Breaking Free from Shyness, Insecurity & Shame to Self Care, Self Acceptance & Self Esteem"

Introduction

I want to thank you and praise you for purchasing the book, *"Self Confidence."* This was a big step to take. You are essentially declaring that enough is enough and it's time to live life confidently!

This book contains proven steps and strategies on how to improve your self-confidence and self-esteem. As with anything in life, there are hurdles that appear along the way such as insecurity and pessimism. This book will teach you exactly how to combat these problems that unexpectedly cross our path on this journey of life.

The beauty of this book lies in its practicality and depth of information based on years of research, experience, and observation on actual events. The well structured chapters inspire us to look at the beauty of life and consider the reasons why we need to be happy, contented and confident with what we have.

My goal is for this book to convince you that you are a unique, amazing, fantastic human being. Consequently, you should be treated as such. When you grasp your inherent value as a person, others will learn to appreciate who you are and what you can do.

I sincerely thank you for purchasing this book and trusting the process of change. I, too, have struggled with constant, unrelenting insecurities, and I appreciate the challenge of conquering these deep rooted beliefs and behaviors. I really hope you enjoy this book and receive great victory!

Chapter 1 - Overcoming Shyness

Sad to say, there are people around us who find it too easy to judge other people based on their list of stereotypes or common categories of people that are deeply embedded in their minds. These preconceived ideas or judgments cloud their perception therefore causing many people to become victims of unfair labeling. Most of the people wrongly judged and labeled by others are those who are shy, worrisome, and insecure. I, too, have been prey to this habit of judgment. It's a belittling, devaluing feeling. It feels unfair and unjust to be labeled in such a way. In this chapter, several techniques on how to overcome these traits will be discussed.

But first, we will begin with the practical remedies for shyness. While people may be born inherently introverted, they can learn to "come out of their shell" and stretch their comfort zone. Give the following remedies a try in order to exercise your confidence muscle.

Shyness Remedy #1: Try to start a conversation with everyone

Experts say that in order to overcome one's shyness, he should make it a point to begin or initiate a conversation with all the people around him. While others argue that it requires confidence to do this, it is said that this very remedy will also address the issue on confidence. You need to practice being confident. If you don't "feel" like it, pretend you are. The feelings of confidence usually follow suit. If you are not yet very confident with yourself, how you look, and what you know, you can learn a lot from conversations. Don't be afraid – you don't have to start with big conversations. You can begin with simple greetings like, "Good day" and "Hello." Start small. Strike up a conversation with the grocery store cashier, the Starbucks barista, the mail carrier or the bus driver.

The more you exercise your muscle, the stronger it will grow. You can slowly add something to the greeting and further substantiate your conversations. Here's another trick: go out of your comfort zone. Move on to more daring acts like approaching the presenter at a conference, the person next to you at McDonald's or a random stranger at a party. Talk to different kinds of people – people from all sectors of society and from all ages.

Take the initiative and talk freely. Don't worry if you stutter or don't sound eloquent. You're practicing. Besides, other people don't notice these things and you'll never have to see them again anyway. Furthermore, you may be surprised by how much you learn about other people and about yourself. As a result, you will learn more about the world around you during your encounters with other people. This will build a repertoire of information that you can use for future conversations. On top of it all, the best reward from all this experience is that you have the potential to acquire new friends.

Shyness Remedy #2: Gather information, learn, and become more educated

Check out the rest of this book on Amazon.

Or go to: http://amzn.to/1aOH5ST

Manipulation

How to Have Healthy Relationships with Controlling People and Reclaim Control of Your Life

Jessica Minty

Table Of Contents

Introduction

I want to thank you and congratulate you for purchasing this book.

This book contains proven steps and strategies on how to recognize manipulators, reclaim your control, set boundaries, and maintain a healthy relationship with them.

The tricky part of manipulation is its subtlety. You will not feel or know that you are being manipulated, if you are not careful. Learn the art of recognizing whether you are being manipulated or if you yourself are a manipulator. Be free from the hold of manipulators and start living your life the way you want.

Thanks again for purchasing this book. I truly hope you feel empowered and free to enjoy your relationships. Please take some time to stop by and LIKE our Facebook page:

https://www.facebook.com/joypublishing

With gratitude,

Jessica Minty

Chapter 1 - The Origin of Manipulation

Manipulation is all about influencing others in order to benefit oneself. Everyone is guilty of this motive. In some way or another, whether directly or indirectly, you have manipulated someone or you were manipulated.

It is human nature to want people to follow you or do things that would benefit you. The only time that this becomes unhealthy is when one starts to make manipulation as part of his/her lifestyle, and in such a way that others are trapped in this web of control. Before learning about the components of manipulation, you need to bear in mind these three very important facts:

1. ***The keyword for manipulation is* subtle**. Because of this, manipulation becomes very hard to recognize. The ones being manipulated may not even feel manipulated at all. In most cases, these people feel that they are just being helpful or generous and would do anything to meet the requests of the person. Most of the time, they feel pity for the person manipulating them. This is a trap. The manipulators know which strings to pull. They know your weaknesses and they will use these against you.

   Are the manipulators aware of what they are doing? Some studies show that some are sincerely not aware that they are being manipulative. Only when they are confronted do they realize that they have crossed the line. From being persuasive they've become manipulative. Having you agree with them was not their main plan.

Most manipulators, however, are aware of their controlling attitude. They actually study you and use the tactic they think you would fall for. Their main goal is to have you say "yes" to all their whims, however irrational those may be.

The way out of this trap is awareness. You need to recognize the strategies being used to manipulate you and think about the best ways of dealing with them.

2. ***You encounter manipulation everyday***. Believe it or not, you participate in manipulation every day of your life. Sometimes, you are the one being manipulated and at other times, you are the one manipulating. This is a fact of life. This is typically harmless unless the will of other people end up being greatly compromised. An example is when you are in a shop and the salesclerk is trying to convince you to buy. The salesclerk can use flattery, which is a form of manipulation. Sometimes, you feel that you are being manipulated but since you truly like the shirt, you let that form of manipulation pass. There is no real harm done. Other times, you are bullied into buying something you do not really want. That is the unhealthy type of manipulation, which needs to be dealt with and put a stop to. Whenever you feel that you are forced into doing something that you feel uncomfortable about, be aware that the manipulator is doing his job.

3. ***Manipulation is a thing of emotion; therefore, the best defense against it is being unemotional***. What is the best way to deal with manipulation? Be very

unemotional about it. The manipulators understand that once they can get you to emotionally agree with them, they've hooked you at last. Do not give them an inch. They'll surely choose to take a mile. Always be on the lookout for the involvement of your emotions. Not to sound callous but being unemotional not only helps you escape their claws, you also help them overcome their very destructive ways.

How did this start?

If ever there would be a law making manipulation a crime, everybody would be condemned. Everybody has participated in this activity at some point in his/her life. You may not be even aware you were doing it. Maybe it is innate to humanity. Maybe it's instinct to try to influence others to have your way. Is it also possible that you were taught into doing this? Let's try to analyze the origin of manipulation.

Is it inborn? Is it learned or acquired?

Remember when you were a child? The only way you can communicate with those around you was by crying. That would cause your parents to assess what you need and satisfy that need. Later on, when you were a little older, you discovered that crying was still effective in having your needs and wants met. So, you cried when you wanted something. You cried when you wanted to be noticed. The message that you received was you could have whatever you want when you cried.

Crying has become a weapon. You grew a little bit more and you added tantrums to crying. For some, that works magic. You have guaranteed success each time. A little more time and you are finally in the adult stage. Although tantrums and loud cries seldom work in the adult phase, tears can still perform their job, no matter how silent they are.

Erik Erickson, author of *Psychosocial Theory*, reinforced this belief in his diagram. Erik theorized that from birth to one year old, the child thought that he was a part or an attachment of the primary caregiver (or most of the time, the mother). As early as 1-3 years old, when the child discovers that he is a separate entity from the caregiver, he assumes full authority of himself, making "No" his favorite word. The basic behavior being developed at this age is willpower or self-control. He wants to be autonomous at all times. Autonomy is not a negative thing. You also want the child to become independent and assertive in life. Without proper guidance, though, autonomy could produce a manipulator.

This is a very delicate stage in the child's life. The parents or the caregiver plays a big role in developing the behavior of the child. The response of the parents or the caregivers to the child's exertion of control over them could shape the behavior of the child at this age and until adulthood. There are three possible responses of parents to the child's efforts to establish control. Let's say, for example, that they are in a toyshop and the child wants that big and expensive toy. The parents said that they are not going to buy it or maybe next time; thus, the child starts to act out, shout, cry loudly, or throw a tantrum and lie on the floor.

The three possible responses of the parents are:

First, give in to the behavior and buy the toy even though they cannot afford it, and that's why they didn't want to buy it in the first place. The child is making a scene and they feel embarrassed. This will strengthen the negative behavior. The next time the child wants another toy, he would know what to do. He learned the art of being a manipulator at an early age.

Second, the parents could get angry and scold the child or even spank the child. This could inhibit the assertiveness of the child and he could grow up and have doubts about himself and his ability. He would just shut up and not verbalize what he wants because he would associate that to being hurt. He learned the role of being a victim to a manipulator.

Third, and this is the recommended action of most psychologists, talk to the child about why you are not going to buy the toy; but at the same time, confirm your love for him. When the child acts out to take control, ignore the behavior but attend to the child's safety and needs. He will eventually grow tired of crying. He will learn not to manipulate. Allow the child to choose and express what he wants through appropriate ways, teaching the child that he can be assertive, but respectful of others, at the same time.

It could be instinct or acquired but the fact remains: everybody has the tendency to influence the decisions of others to benefit themselves. An appropriate response by the individual upon becoming aware of this activity is to drop the manipulating schemes. A man knows that he could influence the person by manipulation in one day or more, but he knows too that is not a real accomplishment, and that, in itself, is a failure. You cannot gain a real friend by being a manipulator. Be a real person and win real friends.

Chapter 2 - -One Side of the Coin

There are always two sides to the coin when it comes to manipulation. One side is the manipulator and the other side is the one being manipulated. They say it takes two to tango. If there would be no permission to be manipulated, then there would be no manipulator. If there were no manipulator, then there would be no victim. It's a cycle and it has to stop.

The problem lies in the subtlety of manipulation. It is not too obvious that would cause people to be wary. More often than not, the victim would not notice it, especially if the issue is not that serious or big. Manipulators are not easy to spot.

The thing with expert manipulators is that they can even make it look like it was you who need to change, that something is wrong with you. Many have fallen for this deception and they have become co-dependent with the manipulators. It is very subtle and tricky, so watch out.

How to determine if a person's a manipulator? Here are some clues.

1. ***Some are very controlling***. Whether by very subtle ways or by means of intimidation, manipulators want to take control of your decision, of your time, and even of your finances. They could be very persistent and creative in their ways of influencing you. Sometimes, they would look for your weaknesses and if they have not found it yet, they would use different strategies to get you to say "yes" to them. Usually, what works best is their politeness and

seemingly good mannered personality. They could impose on you, without you noticing anything.

Their first target is to get you to agree with them on an emotional level. If they could have your "yes," then they could have you. This could be achieved by flattering you, lying to you, or making you feel guilty. Manipulators are good at recognizing their potential victims. They have many strategies to win you over. Be sensitive to the approaches being done to you. You would notice that they are changing their tactics and observing you at the same time. They don't usually stop unless you agree with them or you blatantly say "no" and stand firm with your decision.

2. ***Are always in need and are very dependent***. Most of them appear so helpless that you'll want to lend a hand and just help them out. They have the skill to set you up so that you would help them even without them asking. You would even have the burden to deliver them from their current challenges, as if their survival is in your hands alone.

They tend to be very dependent on you, too. They would have difficulty doing things without you. However, you will notice that after the task is done, these people also disappear. Most of the time, they give no appreciation or show little recognition of the help that you gave. There would be no "Thank you" on their end. You don't have to worry, though. They are bound to come back and seek your help, just give them a couple of days or weeks.

3. ***Some love themselves too much.*** They are narcissists. It is always about them. How they feel, what they need, what they want. It would never be about other people or yourself. They feel that you owe it to them that you are able to do what they need you to do. They are downright using you and they are not ashamed about it. They feel they are too superior to you and it is but natural that you serve them or fulfill their every need.

These manipulators are very skilled in making you feel so low that it would be an honor to serve them. They also have no concern about your feelings and they are not sorry about anything. They love an audience who would adore them and treat them like kings and queens. These are quite easy to recognize but most of the time, these are the master manipulators. Not letting them have control over you could be a real struggle. They don't give up easily, too.

4. ***They act as the martyrs.*** These manipulators are very good at turning the tables. They would act as though they are sacrificing for your benefit, when in fact it's the other way around. They always seem to be doing things for other people but never for themselves. They are always the underdogs, the nobodies, the poor unknown beings that are tread upon by others.

This type of drama elicits pity from other people and makes them emotionally attached to these manipulators. They would feel that they owe so much to the manipulators and they would try to return the favor, when all along, it was just a trap to lure them into having feelings of eternal gratitude. Take note that with this type, you would always feel guilty. You would feel that you have let them, the heroes, down every time you try to refuse their requests. Moreover, they would make sure that you feel and understand that it was you who caused them so much pain.

I, personally, fall into the trap often. There are many times when I find myself in an argument with my husband because he is at fault about something. However, the tables turn and now I'm suddenly the one in "trouble." It gets super confusing and frustrating when this happens. I have to remind myself not to get caught up in his whirlpool of emotions. This is when I need to be careful not to fall into codependency. Check out my codependency book, "Codependency" to learn more about this complex topic.

5. ***Some feign illnesses***. To gain the sympathy of other people, this type of manipulator would always act sick or weak. You would know that this is behavior is fake when the desired thing is given. The sickness vanishes into thin air, like magic. The sickness would strike again when they want another thing done for them.

You see this behavior in children, as well. You can often spot a manipulative temper tantrum versus one that is a complete emotional shutdown. The manipulative temper tantrum is quickly resolved the second the child gets what they want. It's amazing how quickly those tears disappear when they get that ice cream cone or toy. The best way to deal with this kind of temper tantrum is to ignore it the best you can and not fuel the fire. They will quickly learn that this behavior doesn't get them anywhere.

Legitimate temper tantrums are harder to stop because the child is overwhelmed with emotion. The child receiving the object of their desire doesn't necessarily stop the tantrum. Their motive, at this point is not to be manipulative. Their brain is legitimately flooded with emotion and there is no way to rationalize with them. The best way to deal with this kind of temper tantrum is to appeal to their right side, emotional side, of their brain. By empathizing, acknowledging and labeling the way they are feeling, they are able to first calm down. Once they calm down, you are able to speak logic to their left side of the brain.

Some manipulators are very good at faking illness, so you would not know if they are just acting or if it's the real thing. Take the benefit of the doubt when it comes to their sickness. However, do try to find out whether they are really sick. Check their vital signs. They could act well but their bodies would not be able to lie.

6. ***Most are very selfish***. Manipulators think of no one but themselves. Who could help them, who could do the task for them, who could support them – they would never ever consider what they could do for other people. That is so alien to them. They don't really care for the welfare of others, even of those who are helping or supporting them.

You would be able to hear that in their conversation. Their most favorite pronouns are I, me, mine, and myself. The only time they would try to talk about other people is when they have something negative to say about them. Remember, if they could do these to others, they could also do those to you. So, do not encourage them to badmouth other people. Cut the conversation short.

Chapter 3 - -The Other Side of the Coin

Sometimes you are already being manipulated and you are not even aware of it, especially if the manipulator is an expert already. Always be on the lookout. Don't become the next target of these manipulators.

Here are some ways to determine if you are being manipulated.

1. ***You feel guilty every time you have to deny a request or refuse to do something for the person.*** You feel that you owe it to that person to be at his/her side all the time and when something stops you from being there, you feel so guilty. Even when the reason for denying the request is valid (example, you are sick), he/she could end up as being the neglected one because of your absence. Though you have always given the person your best, he or she has a way of making you feel that you did not give your best. You just don't love him/her enough.

2. ***You feel forced to do something you do not want to do.*** Although you have exerted effort not to be pushed into something you do not feel comfortable with, you still end up doing exactly that. This is the skilled motivator at work against you. They can make something look like it was your idea in the first place when, in truth, you don't even want to do anything with it. It usually dawns on you too late. During the actual "transaction," you have the strength to refuse and then later on, you just find yourself agreeing to their suggestions. Afterwards, you would feel bad about being forced into that particular thing.

15

If the one who manipulated you is not a friend, you would not come back to that shop or place again. However, if the person whom you believe manipulated you is a friend, you would end up being extra careful when interacting with that friend the next time around. It's also possible that you would not even want to be in that person's company again.

3. **You can't say no**. Even though you know the answer should be "no," you end up saying "yes". The manipulator always tries to get his/her way all the time. It does not matter if you have more important things to do, his/her request is always more important. If you notice that you have not refused an acquaintance at any time, assess carefully. Maybe you are already being manipulated.

   Be sensitive also on the tactics being used on you. Initially, manipulators would be so sweet and convincing. It would really be hard to say "no" to them. However, if you still refuse, they would use another strategy, like making you feel guilty about your decision. It's also true that some use anger and intimidation. You'll find out that they have so many strategies hidden up their sleeves.

4. **You feel it's your fault, all the time**. Something went wrong, so it was your fault. The weather was bad, and so it was your fault. He/she was not hired, so it was your fault. Every single negative thing is your fault. He or she is not even saying it. You feel it yourself. You have been brainwashed into thinking that the manipulator can never

be wrong. Even why you are being manipulated is your fault. You caused them to be like that.

The manipulators are blind to their weaknesses and faults. They love the blame game.

5. **You feel selfish**. Why are you always thinking about yourself? If you catch yourself thinking like this, beware. You might have fallen into the trap. Again, they are experts in reversing things. They are the ones who are truly selfish, but they can make you as if you are the selfish one. If, for example, you want to take a break and be with your friends, they would capitalize on that and make you feel like you are a bad person. You won't be able to think of having fun.

The easiest way to detect manipulation is to check yourself. If, at any time, you realize you were forced to do something or you feel guilty and bad about yourself when you know you shouldn't be, then it's time to expose manipulation and put a stop to it. If not, it will take control of your life, completely.

Chapter 4 - -How to Reclaim Control Over Your Life

Admit it. You feel that you would never fall into the trap of manipulators. You think that it only happens in the movies or to your friends, but never to you. You feel so lost, you cannot think of how and why you reached this point. You have totally lost control over your own life!

You feel ashamed of yourself. You lost the esteem and confidence you once had. You are so mad at yourself for not recognizing it too soon. You are also so mad at the manipulators. You think all is gone.

The good news is, it's not yet too late. Everything can be recovered. Yes, even your life. How exactly would you do that? Here are some ways to reclaim control over your life.

1. ***Realize you were manipulated***. The most difficult thing to accept is that you were manipulated. This is simply because the tactics were so subtle. You did not notice it. You think nothing was wrong or amiss. You sometimes even think that it was your fault why you were being controlled by your friend or partner. Maybe there is indeed, something wrong with you.

   Acceptance that you were victimized is the first step towards recovery. As long as you think you are not being manipulated, you will not be able to get out of the trap. Once you become aware that you lost the control to run your life and that someone else is running your life for his or her benefit, then the start of your freedom has come.

You must make the decision to put a stop to this. You have to be deliberate. Forgive yourself. Do not blame yourself for what happened.
Take this as a lesson. The next time there is somebody who would try to manipulate you again, you would recognize the tactics easily and you will not fall into the trap again.

2. ***Forgive the person.*** Do not be bitter about what happened. You need to let go and move on. Not able to forgive is an expensive deal. You are on the losing end. You do not have to tell the person all the wrongs that he or she has done to you. Anyway, most of the time, they do not realize the effect they have had on you. Realize that in the end, the manipulators are the real victims. Their lives are not really that happy. They have no real success. Sadly, they have no real friends.

3. ***Have time for yourself and away from that person.*** Create some space if possible. Stay away from the person if you can. Just in case that would be impossible, like it's your parents and you are the one taking care of them, try to maintain distance while you heal. Having time for yourself would also help you reflect on what has transpired and what can be done in the future. Be ready though. At this time, you should expect the manipulators to win you at all cost. They would seek your attention and presence at all times. They would do anything to have you

back. Be firm and establish yourself first before you face them again. You will need it if you don't ever want to be trapped again.

4. ***Boost your self-confidence and self-esteem.*** Manipulators are very good in making you feel inadequate, as if you're a loser. You were always thinking of their wellbeing, but you have totally neglected yours. This time, take charge. Take care of yourself. Value yourself once more. Do not let this encounter change you into a lesser person. Do the things that you want and without feeling guilty. Buy the things that you need and do not be pressured into thinking that you are being selfish. Have that trip, or have that vacation. You totally deserve it.

You may have been fooled into thinking that you are not smart or successful, but you can reclaim your confidence and self-esteem. Realize this – if they are the manipulators, it simply means they are the losers. They are the ones with low self-esteem. That's why they resorted to manipulation.

I believe my book, "Self Confidence" will really boost your self esteem and help you conquer insecurity.

5. ***Do not be manipulated again.*** Be careful not to fall into the trap again. They are very good in courting you back again with flowers, tears, and promises. Consistency and firmness on your part are very crucial at this time. Do not be swayed by their charms once again. Always remember

that you have no power to change them. Only they can help themselves.

Chapter 5 - How to Have a Healthy Relationship With Manipulators?

There are cases when it would be best to leave the manipulators and have nothing to do with them ever again, especially if it is an intimate relationship. But tread lightly. This is not an easy decision to make and it could affect the lives of many, most importantly, children. Accept that you cannot change them. The changes would have to come through their own efforts.

However, if your situation calls for you to continue a relationship with them (such as in the case of manipulative parents, partners or employers), then setting boundaries is a must for you!

What are boundaries?

You would set these limits so that the manipulators cannot do their stuff on you. In other words, they would not be able to control you anymore. It is a list of the things that you are willing to allow, but only up to certain points only. Other than that, it's either they comply with your boundaries or leave you alone. This time, it's your call. It is you who is in charge.

Be aware that when you first start setting your boundaries, you will experience push back from the other person. They are used to you behaving in a certain way. Now that you are affirming yourself, they are going to respond negatively until they get used to the new you.

With my father, I set boundaries by making sure I'm not alone with him. I try to go to his house rather than him come to mine because I can leave whenever I want to.

Reasons for Boundaries

Before you set the boundaries, there are things you need to know. Boundaries are designed to protect you and the relationship. It is not another form of manipulation with you being the manipulator. That is not the reason for creating boundaries. You set up boundaries to let the manipulators know that you care for yourself and you would not allow them to manipulate you anymore. Boundaries are not threats to be used against them, too. Boundaries are essentially a decision, a choice that you would have to make if they would not change.

Win the battle by being unemotional

Again, manipulation is a battle that primarily involves your emotions. Do you remember the most important way of dealing with manipulation? Be unemotional about it. You have to separate yourself with your feelings to do what you know is right for everybody. Make your list of boundaries without relying on your emotions. After making your list, present that to the manipulators, emphasizing that you would really abide by it and you expect them to do the same. Be non-accusatory. Just stay objective. Be aware that this is where the real drama could begin. They may shed tears and start bargaining. They may tell you to be merciful and that they would not be able to survive your boundaries. They could also be very mad and would not even allow you to finish your discussion. It is okay. The next important thing is to stick to your decision to abide in your boundaries.

The formula for setting boundaries

So, how do you set boundaries? You could follow this formula – "If you____," followed by the manipulative act, "then I will ____," followed by an action or response. For example, "if you verbally abuse me again (like calling me stupid or loser), I will leave the room or house, I would even have to ask you to leave." Focus on the behavior, not on the person. Be specific so that the manipulators would be aware of what is expected from them. The boundaries should be very clear. They should know what is acceptable to you or not. You should not feel apologetic because of your boundaries. Most importantly, make sure you follow through! The worst think you can do is be inconsistent. You must back up your boundaries with action.

The real key, however, is not the list but the implementation. Tests coming from the side of the manipulator would happen. Be ready for that. However, if you would stick to your boundaries, there will come a time that they would stop manipulating you. They know it is not going to work with you anymore.

Again, be very unemotional about the manipulators. That is their primary target – your emotions. Do not let them have the upper hand using your emotions. It is not that you do not care. In fact, it is because you care about yourself and them that you would not rely on emotions in dealing with this.

Chapter 6 - -The Real Deal

Manipulation is a game that you do not need to become a part of. It is a form of addiction that's hard to get out of once you are in. Sometimes, you think it's just cute and sweet to manipulate by doing this – I'll give you a super kiss if you buy me that outfit. That is harmless manipulation. Friends sometimes manipulate their own friends and they know it, but they do it just the same. You sometimes let yourself be manipulated by friends. It's because those are your friends and you know them well. The act of manipulation becomes unhealthy when it becomes a lifetime of coercion, or force comes into the picture. At that point, it is time to deal with it.

There is life outside manipulation. If you ever find yourself using manipulation to have others agree with you, stop the act immediately. You would not want to be among the manipulators. They have no real life. They have no real friends.

On the other hand, once you realize that you are being manipulated, act immediately to put a stop to it. Do not give them anything to work on, not even an inch.

The real thing

There is a beautiful life outside of manipulation. This should be the target. This is the real deal. Having someone agree with you just because you manipulated him or her is not a real win. That is a sad attempt to establish control. Yes, you would temporarily feel that you have won, and that you were successful. The end result would determine the real deal. If they feel coerced, forced, or controlled, you have not gained anything. You have lost the respect and trust of those people.

You can have influence over others without the use of manipulation. Just be the real you. Being you is the real deal. Being true is the real deal.

Conclusion

Thank you again for purchasing *"Manipulation."*

I hope this book was able to help you to understand manipulation and how to handle it.

The next step is to stop the hold of manipulation on you and start living the life that you want.

Finally, if you enjoyed and appreciated this book, please take the time to share your thoughts and post a positive review on Amazon. It'd be greatly appreciated!

I truly hope my experiences and stories brought you encouragement. I would love for you to share your experiences, stories and encouragements with me. My email address is jessicamintykindle@gmail.com

In addition, please remember to check out our Facebook page in order to find other resources and upcoming promotions:

https://www.facebook.com/joypublishing

With sincere thanks,

Jessica Minty

Preview of "Mindfulness Meditation: Mindfulness & Anxiety Management for Overcoming Anxiety & Worry to Emotional Health, Inner Peace & Happiness"

Chapter 1

The Basics of Mindfulness: Discovering What Your Mind Can Do

The famous saying "What your mind can conceive, your body can achieve" has been extensively used in order to motivate people to pursue whatever their goal is. This is because if their mind is set on a single goal, the body will be directed as to what actions must be taken to achieve it. Fortunately, this saying is also applicable in helping us cope with problems and invite positive vibes in our life.

This chapter aims to discover the basics of mindfulness – what it is, and how its practice can lead to a better life.

What is mindfulness?

Mindfulness is a form of meditation which aims to become aware of your feelings, sensations, and thoughts while you are in a non-judgmental and relaxed state. In a simpler sense, its aim is to know what's going on with yourself internally and in the present moment. When a person is mindful, they are able to see everything around them naturally, and are not concerned with what or how things should be.

Mindfulness is said to be similar to a Buddhist meditation practiced that was started around 2500 years ago. However, mindfulness is not a religiously connected meditation method, and every person regardless of their religious affiliation can practice it.

A majority of the time, our brain functions on auto pilot when we go about our daily actions. This is a very efficient tool that the brain uses. However, so often we find ourselves behaving in ways that don't line up with what we value. I'm constantly caught in the trap of where I know I want to be and what I'm actually doing in the present moment. I get so frustrated with myself when my behaviors don't line up with my values. Why is it that I want to do "good", but I can't? When I don't want to do "bad," I do it anyway? How annoying this cycle is for me.

Fortunately, the brain is smart and knows that it doesn't always get it right. That's why it give us consciousness so we can interrupt the process and turn off the auto pilot. Mindfulness is actually the key to turning the auto pilot off and enhancing your ability to recognize what your brain is doing.

There are so many fantastic benefits to mindfulness meditation. This is actually a really exciting time for mindfulness and science. Research on the incredibleness of mindfulness is increasing rapidly because scientists are realizing how pivotal mindfulness is on our brain health. It won't be long before mindfulness sky rockets through the population and everyone will be doing it. It's kind of like how yoga became popular and little yoga studios popped up everywhere. In the same way, I believe that mindfulness will be taught in schools and there will also be studios popping up around the city. It will become common place, as it should.

Could you imagine if they actually taught this stuff in school? I'm a teacher so I get really fired up about this. I teach practical life skills to my students and now where in the curriculum is such a beneficial and life altering skill taught. If people were educated on how to deal with stress, anger, depression, cravings, etc, our world would be such a different place. Ooooh, it gets me excited at the possibilities of what could be. That's why this book is so important to me.

So what are its benefits?

The following benefits can be experienced by people who practice mindfulness:

- It can help lower stress – applying mindfulness in daily situations has been found to lower stress. When a person is in the state of mindfulness, they are more able to determine the root cause of their problem. It will also help them to prioritize which problem should be attended to first. As their mind becomes open to their problems without negative thoughts, better solutions can be conceived. Ultimately, this will lead to solving the whole problem.

- It can help prevent depression and anxiety – some people are easily overwhelmed when they are faced with problems that seem to stack one after another. As you are able to prioritize which problems should be solved first by applying mindfulness, the feeling that you can't get over them will eventually fade away. Similarly, the feeling of depression is also reduced. After all, the more control you have with the situation, the less anxious and the more emotionally stable you are.

- It can help improve your physical health – it is common for meditation methods to include relaxation techniques. Deep breathing and getting calm, some of the behaviors observed in meditation methods, are known to improve heart rate and lower blood pressure.

- It can improve your memory and mental functions – surprisingly, mindfulness can also enhance a person's memory. This is because mindfulness requires you to recall every possible situation that you've experienced during the day. You are also forced to think of every possible solution to situations that are causing you problems. As you use your brain more, your mental function will improve as well. The process of mindfulness actually rewires the brain. Studies on the brain show incredible improvements to the brain in as short as two weeks!

- It helps you see the situation on a new light – even the worst possible situation that you can ever think of has a silver lining. Either there is a meaning behind it, or there is a lesson that you can learn from it. With the help of mindfulness, it becomes easier to see the problem in another perspective. This in turn will help you to become more positive in dealing with the problem and avoid having negative feelings about it.

- It curbs your cravings – mindfulness practices have been used to control food cravings and even strong emotions. The SOBER technique, which will be shared later, is a fantastic technique that comes out on top through research studies on cravings.

- It builds self confidence and self acceptance – mindfulness notices our thoughts for what they are: neutral. There are no "good" or "bad" thoughts. Just thoughts. The problem is when we show up and attach meaning to those thoughts. But mindfulness just lets those thoughts float through our mind and not attach meaning to them. As quickly as those thoughts come is as quickly as they leave. I found this concept profound and it really clicked with me. Many years ago, when I was wrestling with postpartum depression, I learned about this concept in counseling. I so often would have bombarding thoughts that would go through my mind that I associated as negative. As a result, I would beat myself up for having those thoughts and label myself in negative ways. However, when I learned that I can just let my thoughts pass through my mind without having any attachment to who I was as a person – I was set free! What a relief for me. I continue to practice this concept to this day.

- It enhances willpower – willpower is a key factor in the quality and length of our life. It behaves like a muscle that needs to get exercised in order to grow bigger. We all know that our lives would be so much more successful if we actually did the behaviors that we know we should. More often than not, we don't because we aren't disciplined enough to follow through. Consequently, we've developed a habit of not doing rather than a habit of doing. Mindfulness meditation is one of the best ways that you can drastically improve your willpower. Research studies show that the improvements to our brain are almost instantaneous! Chapter 3 continues talking about willpower and I have a book dedicated to it: "Willpower Guide."

- It increases your heart rate variability – your heart rate variability is connected with your willpower. Science is also zeroing in its affects in our body. So far, we know that our heart rate variability communicates how much willpower is at our disposal. Obviously, the wider our heart rate variability, the better our willpower will be. Meditation is one of the best methods for enhancing your heart rate variability. The effects in studies are shown to be almost immediate. Again, I talk more about heart rate variability, and what to do/not do in "Willpower Guide." Another resource for you to use is www.heartmath.org. You just need to type in "heart rate variability" into their search engine.

Why mindfulness is not that easy?

Since mindfulness shares the same practices observed in other meditation techniques, you might think that it is not that difficult to apply. This belief, however, is false. This is because the following issues are experienced by people who practice mindfulness:

- Some of your expectations may not be met – people who start applying mindfulness meditation usually have low expectations at first. But as they continue to engage in this activity for quite some time, their expectation of the occurrence of results increases. After all, they've given enough time and opportunity for this method to show results, and it is natural for people to expect results from something that they've spent their time on. Unfortunately, mindfulness is not similar to prescription medicine, since it never gives results immediately. Even if the goal of mindfulness is to provide the benefits stated above, there is no definite schedule as to when its effects will be experienced. If expectations are not met, there is a huge tendency that the person will stop meditating, with the belief that this method "does not work". Although you may not yet see changes, know that your brain and heart chemistry immediately react, as proven by scans during research.

- Its practice can make you feel uncomfortable – when a person starts meditation, they can either be physically uncomfortable, or their thoughts may cause them discomfort.

a. Being physically uncomfortable – in this form of meditation, you are required to remain in a seated position or in other comfortable position. However, getting uncomfortable cannot be avoided, especially if you have to maintain the said position for a significant amount of time. Although being aware of what your body is experiencing can be a part of the routine, these issues can be significant enough and may interrupt your meditation.

b. Getting uncomfortable with your thoughts – when a person is not in motion, his or her mind will bring into consciousness different ideas or thoughts. Although having more of these thoughts are beneficial in formulating solutions to your problems, the surge of ideas can also create more confusion as to which is the best solution for your problem. Simply put, it can slow down their pace when making decisions. There will also be instances when undesirable thoughts surface as the meditation continues, which can become distracting if they follow through it. And even if the meditation was stopped due to the continuous re-surfacing of the undesirable thought, the fact that it was brought into awareness can make it difficult for you to forget about it. There is a risk that you'll be adding another problem that you have to solve.

Although it can be hard to start, it's important to start. Habits take at least 21 days to form. This is definitely a habit you want to form! Start small on a daily basis. Begin with 3 minutes and work your way up to 10 or 15 minutes or longer. Don't beat yourself up if you are unable to commit to 10 – 15 minutes. It is better to have a short meditation practice than none at all. You will still acquire the profound benefits.

Check out the rest of this book on Amazon

Or go to: http://amzn.to/1JtJNZi

Check Out My Other Books

Below you'll find some of my other books also available on Amazon and Kindle. Search for these titles on Amazon to find them.

Anxiety Relief: Breaking Free from Shyness, Insecurity & Shame to Self Care, Self Acceptance& Self Esteem

http://amzn.to/1FomK3z

Codependency: A Relationship Rescue for Toxic Relationships, Manipulation & Enabling to Self Confidence, Boundaries, Emotional Health & Happiness ****BEST SELLER**

http://amzn.to/1DpogQQ

EFT Tapping: Emotional Freedom to Break Free From Cravings, Temptation & Bad Habits to Emotional Health, Stress Relief & Happiness

http://amzn.to/1NXiAyQ

Jealousy: A Relationship Rescue for Overcoming Fear, Insecurity, Trust Issues, Lying & Envy to Trust & Healthy Relationships

http://amzn.to/1DNE2a1

Manipulation: A Relationship Rescue for Breaking Free from Bad Relationships, Mind Control, Emotional Abuse & Codependency to Reclaiming Your Self Confidence & Sanity

http://amzn.to/1CAe2YE

Mindfulness Meditation: Mindfulness & Anxiety Management for Overcoming Anxiety & Worry to Emotional Health, Inner Peace & Happiness

http://amzn.to/1JtJNZi

Perfectionism: Letting Go of Mistakes & Overcoming Anxiety, Perfection & Procrastination to Victory &Self Acceptance

http://amzn.to/1Fon0PZ

Self Confidence: Breaking Free from Shyness, Insecurity & Shame to Self Care, Self Acceptance& Self Esteem

http://amzn.to/1aOH5ST

Willpower: Breaking Free From Cravings, Temptation & Bad Habits to Self Control, Self Discipline& Goal Setting

http://amzn.to/1yhbweN

One Last Thing...

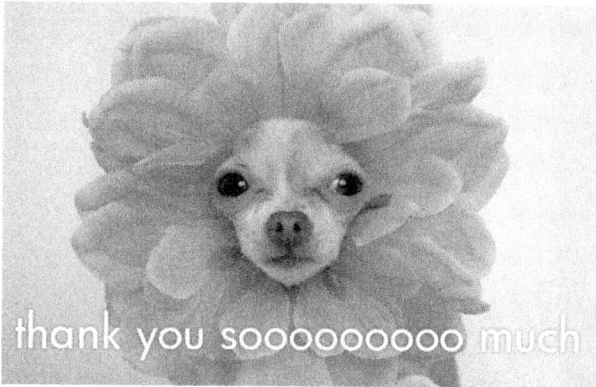

If you believe that this book is worth sharing, would you please take the time to let others know how it affected your life? If it turns out to make a difference in the lives of others, they will be forever grateful to you, as will I.

CPSIA information can be obtained at www.ICGtesting.com
Printed in the USA
BVOW06s0235190716

456071BV00023B/168/P